Keep It Real

**Why We're Afraid
To Speak Up,
And
What To Do About It**

Keep It Real

**Why We're Afraid
To Speak Up,
And
What To Do About It**

Mountain Flower

**Pueblo
Press**

Keep It Real
Why We're Afraid To Speak Up And What To Do
About It.

By Mountain Flower/Leslie Karen Hammond

Published by: Pueblo Press
131 Daniel Webster Highway #325
Nashua, NH 03060

Interior Design by Mark Roberts, Pueblo Press

Requests for permission should be sent to:
Pueblo Press
131 Daniel Webster Highway #325
Nashua, NH 03060
860-303-8772

ISBN: 978-0-9836344-2-3

Other books by Mountain Flower/Leslie Karen Hammond

Tap Your Source

Women Rising: How To Go From Uncomfortable To Unstoppable

Holding Space: How To Help Women Feel Safe

Conversational Intelligence: Understanding Your Style To Help Others Feel Heard

Keep It Clean: Energy Clearing and Illumination Exercises for Empaths

Dedication

This book is dedicated to every person who kept quiet because she or he didn't want to make waves.

If you've ever felt like your opinion didn't count, I'm here to tell you it does.

The next time anyone asks you, "Who do you think you are," you will be prepared to answer him or her.

Contents

Acknowledgments

To Wasaka –

Thank you for holding space for me always to speak freely. Not only have I embraced my voice, I've learned to sing.

iv

Preface

Keep It Real is an invitation to acknowledge what keeps you silent. You may not be ready to do anything about your auditory captivity; then again, you may be ready to take a stand. Wherever this book takes you, please know I am with you in Spirit and holding space for your arrival into the best version of you the world has yet to see and hear. Extraordinary things await you when you make the choice to *Keep It Real*.

The intent for this book is to help you understand the emotion behind communication from a deeper perspective. If you've ever been too timid to speak your truth, this book will empower you to speak up and be heard.

When you can clearly see your pattern of communication over a lifetime, this knowledge provides feedback on how you are interpreted by others when you speak.

This book will also invite you to be accountable for how you presently communicate while exploring new talking methods. I aim to have you feel good about what you say, feel heard, and be valued. You no longer need to be kept silent out of a sense of obligation.

"The only person you are destined to become is the person you decide to be."

– Ralph Waldo Emerson

Chapter 1

Are We Born This Way?

As early as my first report card, I recall reading, "Leslie talks too much." Clearly, I had the gift of gab and no desire to filter it. The irony of this early beginning is that for much of my adolescence, I was chastised and never fit in. When I was comfortable, I spoke up.

When I was not, I remained silent. How often was I comfortable, you wonder?

This gift of outspokenness was a fast-burning flame. Between my pixie hairstyle and my corrective shoes (required to turn my feet outward), it didn't take long for me to become increasingly silent in an environment of non-acceptance.

The fear of public speaking hits people so intensely because it's a throwback to standing in front of the classroom delivering a report. Many were ridiculed and not rescued. No one received any training; the teachers threw you to the wolves and insisted you stand in front of the class and speak.

If you're not a fan of public speaking, do you experience this flashback when you need to talk in front of a group? The visceral reaction from your early speaking experiences can be an uncomfortable reminder of a time in your life when you were judged and didn't feel "good enough." So much of my work focuses on reversing the subconscious memory of unworthiness.

You are worthy of being heard, seen, and experienced.   Anyone who tells you otherwise feels threatened by you or doesn't fully understand you.

When people are not supportive, they don't know how to hold the vision of your worthiness. It's out of their realm of experience.   They cannot be accountable for a skill they've never learned; it's a limitation of their conditioning.

Most folks recall their parents telling them not to be concerned with what other people say. Parents tell children to ignore the bullies and walk away, but the fact of the matter is the child had an assault on their self-esteem.

If you got lucky, you identified early with a skill and had the training to develop it further.   You may still have been the outcast of the larger population, but in your small community, you had a place.

For those of you who never found a place, the urge to remain silent for the sake of safety may have become your new "normal." Adopting a wallflower presence may have been a means of survival.

Children who don't experience fitting in usually grow up in one of two ways. Either they become hyper-focused, very successful adults, or rebel to fit in. The more rebellious may turn to destructive behavior. I was initially the latter of the two.

The one good thing that came out of my teenage "destructive" phase was that I'd found my voice again. Call it liquid courage, but I found a way to feel larger than life. The peer-imposed silence lifted, and I felt free.

The vital thing to know about this phase is that it didn't last very long. I matured rather quickly for a rebellious young person.

Now that we've looked at the external forces that keep us silent, let's look at a more internal perspective.

Studies have shown that a child in utero will absorb the survival mechanisms of the parent, most noticeably when extreme circumstances are present. Many children born from parents during WWII had high rates of obesity because of the mother's fear of not having enough to eat. So many of those children became stuck in permanent survival mode.

Before piecing gestational trauma together with the fear of speaking, I'd believed people's resistance was a learned behavior. I also thought this fear was rooted in upbringing, reinforced by who one spent time with as an adult.

A child, in utero, senses the mother's environment. It makes perfect sense that a child feels their mother's emotions.

Looking back at my pregnancy and the drama going on in my life, I must consider how my emotional state impacted my son.

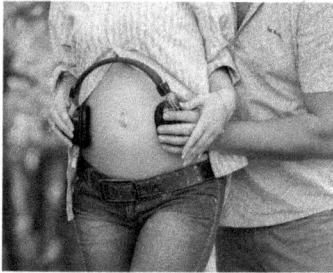

I found out I was pregnant when my husband was in ICU after a motorcycle accident. He had been drinking and had a blood-alcohol level of .27, and rode without a helmet. He was in intensive care for a week and in the hospital for seven weeks. Most of the time, I fell asleep on his hospital bed during my visits after work.

During this period in 1987, I was working 50 hours a week with a one-hour commute. He was collecting unemployment, doing odd jobs, and riding his Harley. I was in love and enamored by my husband's "bad boy" stereotype. If you can envision his light brown, long curly hair and blue-green eyes, you'd understand where my hormones were. To tell the truth, he had saved me from myself a few years earlier, and I had grown accustomed to his protection. What I never got used to was the cost of being controlled.

When released from the hospital, he came home to convalesce. The doctor said it would be a long recovery. In addition to the broken foot, I had to contend with his traumatic brain injury, the exhaustion of the first trimester of pregnancy, and working to support us. My whole pregnancy was about his recovery. No one to dote over the first time mother, it was all about getting through each day. Back then money was so tight I had to make my maternity dresses.

With all the stress I was under, I cannot imagine my son isolated from everything I was feeling. Beyond the emotion pressure, there was the physical tension in my body as well. Every sound in the night had the potential to bring about a mild panic attack. These memories are why I'm such a light sleeper to this day.

Almost three decades later I'm beginning to see the connection between some of my son's sensitivities and my stress during pregnancy.

If you have family members with behaviors you cannot understand, consider looking at the circumstances of their mother's life while she carried the child whose adult behavior you now question.

You may be tempted to judge someone's behavior harshly without understanding the root of the problem. The revelation is by no means the "be all end all" explanation nor an excuse for unacceptable behavior. Your findings may shed some light on unconscious behavior.

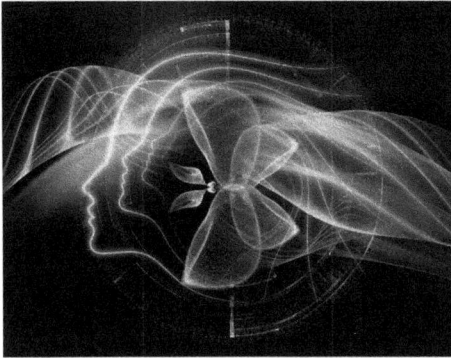

The puzzle comes together when considering these circumstances concerning a person's ability to speak up. What if a mother was always silenced as a child and then married into a controlling relationship? There are minimal references to acting courageously. Just because a mother is accustomed to being silenced does not mean she feels no emotion every time her silencing occurs. Feeling inadequate and insecure is not something the body can ignore. In fact, the body stores these memories long after we think we've left them behind.

Emotionally, people may shut down or compartmentalize unpleasant memories because there is still a visceral reaction within the body. This "muscle memory" cannot be shut off. It may appear as a pit in the stomach from fear or shame. It may show up as a rapid heartbeat preceding a panic attack, a skin disorder, hair falling out, or urinary ailments. Your body will not lie about what you feel.

I no longer believe a person's fear of speaking is strictly a learned tendency.

It's been a privilege to help people remember their ability to speak up. A world of possibility opens the instant you start to see the patterns of silence in a new light. If you'd like some tips on beginning this process, check out my website, www.MTflower.com, or contact me at Hello@MTflower.com.

"Remember, no one can make you feel inferior without your consent."

- Eleanor Roosevelt

Chapter 2

Environment

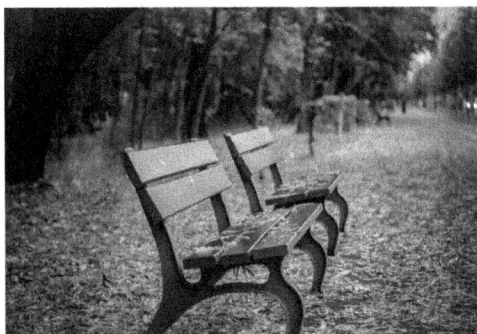

C hapter 1 made reference to the power of fitting in and its importance in self-esteem. The environment is also essential to success. It's important to surround yourself with people who believe in you. With a different perspective on the source of someone's fear of speaking up, let's look at how those concerns continue to manifest.

The people you surround yourself with serve to hold you up and support you. But if you aren't paying attention, they can also be the person who holds you down. The mental, emotional, and physical places you occupy result from many circumstances and individuals who have come into your life.

People who are too intimidated to speak up often surround themselves with people who exhibit the same behavior. You may see people with successful careers who talk as a condition of their employment, but it doesn't mean they are comfortable speaking up about their emotions.

Some of the most aggressive people you know may have poor communication skills in their personal lives. They may put up a wall to protect themselves. It sounds counter-intuitive, but consider this;

When people are assertive, they cannot be vulnerable simultaneously. Assertiveness is an unconscious protective mechanism.

Safety is subjective. People will go to great lengths to ensure the perception of feeling safe. An individual who doesn't want to make waves will quickly retreat.

The surprising fact about the retreat and controlling personality styles is the unconscious level of comfort each has in their role. This co-dependency, although unhealthy, is familiar. Most folks have not developed a taste for the unfamiliar or uncertainty, so they stay with what they know. In unhealthy situations, if you put two of the same personalities together in a relationship, it won't take long for the imbalance to show up.

I've always believed people enter into dominant/submissive relationships because it's what they've experienced as children.

It's familiar territory. There is a part of each of us that sometimes prefers to be told what to do. When we are exhausted, we often don't want to think. This type of surrender comes up for me when I'm too mentally drained to make a decision for myself. Given a choice, I may not have the bandwidth to decide. Apathy takes over, and I take what I get with no argument.

To better understand people who are more comfortable taking direction than giving it, consider looking at it from a "comfort zone" perspective. Giving guidance implies leadership, vision, and management. These qualities are of no interest to people who are content with their lives. Receiving direction requires following instructions, which is easier than thinking out a strategy. There may also be an accountability factor; giving direction makes you accountable for the actions of those you are directing. Most content people don't have this level of accountability.

You are now thinking more about the people in your immediate circle. As you become conscious of people's characteristics, patterns, and behavior, please make every effort to suspend judgment and spare no effort to understand them. Many responses are conditioned. When someone doesn't know how to be supportive in a way you want to experience, they have no history of behaving that way. With no form of reference, people default to what they know.

Part of the problem can be a lack of communication on your part, too.

How often do you convey what you want to feel most supported?

Sometimes, discussion alone is not enough, especially if you haven't selected an optimal moment or the best surroundings to speak up. Frustration will ensue if you explain something and the other party is not committed to understanding what you need. An excellent way to confirm their understanding is by paraphrasing. Ask them to explain in their own words what you meant. If it's still unclear, you'll know and have a chance to take corrective action.

A word of advice when someone does not understand what you mean: resist the need to tell him or her they are wrong.

Take responsibility for not explaining what you meant in a way they could understand and attempt again. I promise this will go a long way. If the other person feels blame coming from you, they will shut down. When they understand what you mean, phrase them generously. Tell them how much you appreciate their listening effort and attention to what you need. Imagine what this can do to the state of a relationship!

Let's circle back to the larger group of people surrounding you. If you want to improve your communication skills, find a group that can support you in this process.

The risk will be well worth the effort. It requires stepping out of your comfort zone. Groups such as Toastmasters International are fantastic; you speak up when you are ready. I've seen people remain silent for weeks, sometimes months before they were ready. The act of getting yourself in an environment of individuals willing to communicate is a great start.

There are also a lot of self-help groups and 12-step programs out there. I'll caution you about these over the long haul. In my experience, the group initially helped, but after a while, I felt stagnant.

Ready to start speaking up? Seek out groups of people who are nurturing and comfortable to be around. You can also take a class at your local community college. Take a look at where you think you'd be most comfortable, then stretch yourself a little.

Without support, the status quo will never change, and disappointment will take over.

As you step into the life you want to lead, your supporters must grow as you grow. The people you surround yourself with will significantly impact your success.

Many marriages end in divorce because people expand their minds and experiences at different rates, or in some cases, only one person grows while the other is happy to remain stagnant. The tension builds as the person growing feels less supported, and the content person begins to feel ignored.

When an individual in transformation does not feel supported, they must possess a commitment more robust than the resistance surrounding them to succeed.

"If you hear a voice within you say, 'You cannot paint,' then by all means, paint, and that voice will be silenced."

-Vincent Van Gogh

Chapter 3

The Inner Critic

The little voice in your head that thinks it knows better and claims it's protecting you from harm is a byproduct of the people who have influenced you. It only takes one naysayer to impact an already delicate ego. My self-esteem issues begin in early childhood. The wrath of judgment from other people started at the tender age of 5. Crying was practically a daily occurrence.

The outcasting continued. I was always the last person standing when kickball teams formed. I was the flat-chested tomboy with no friends. I've never been to a prom or a homecoming.

My parents weren't aware of the pain in my daily life. Like most adolescents, I grew independent in a climate that didn't support it. I'm sure there were some happy times, but I'd be lying if I told you I could remember them.

My inner critic was fed regularly from age five until age fourteen with such a consistency I'm not sure what prompted my revolt. Perhaps marijuana. During those early years, I became difficult to manage, although that time ultimately served a greater purpose. I redefined what it meant to be strong-willed while breaking every rule intended to set me straight. I always believed that by the time I was 18, I had lived more than most people in their 30s.

How this is relevant to my Inner Critic will be apparent in a moment.

I spent a few years flexing my independence muscles, which, to most folks, appeared to be wreaking havoc almost everywhere I went. I had to prove a point, and there'd be no stopping me.

After years of denial and being treated like an outcast, I was going to flex my independence at all costs. I had no regard for anyone but myself. Enter, Patrick.

In all honesty, he saved me from me. Without him, I may have been incarcerated or, worse, dead. Our relationship began as a friendship and grew for two years. I intended to keep it that way. I never had an older brother or a relationship where I felt so safe. I wasn't about to jeopardize this newfound comfort zone. Everything shifted once I agreed to take the relationship to an intimate level. The once independent, untamed soul became submissive and controlled. We remained married for 18 years. He was an alcoholic. You could say I imploded.

Enter my Inner Critic.

Regardless of how unhealthy it is, a familiar situation will almost always trump the fear of the unknown.

I stayed in the marriage for so long because I was convinced I deserved this. Perhaps

I'd done something extreme in a previous life; perhaps it was the pregnancies I'd terminated. Perhaps this was poetic justice - all the cruelty I'd shown my parents was coming back full circle.

I took the role very seriously when I became a mother at 23. I nursed my son for two years. When he began ingesting solid food, it had to be organic. There were no temper tantrums tolerated. I did everything I could to ensure his view of the world was positive and supportive. Granted, I had his father working against me with the drinking, but that only increased my diligence.

I carried my son facing out in a "baby pack," got him into group daycare at six months old, and constantly encouraged him. I refused to let him be the "social refugee" I once was. For my son, I found strength, yet I still settled and endured.

My inner critic was always close; she told me I deserved my situation and I ought to be grateful to others who had it worse. I didn't have it that bad. Clearly, she didn't understand how badly I was deteriorating.

My Inner Critic took decades to get in check because I took a long time to surround myself with people who believed in me.

How many people in your life believe in you? If you can count them on one hand, you are fortunate. If you can count them on two hands, you are truly blessed. Please be sure to tell these people how much you appreciate their support. It is because of them you are where you are. It is because of them you will get where you want to go.

When your Inner Critic needs stricter management, consider surrounding yourself with more people who appreciate you as you are. Seek out individuals who can help you create, support, and sustain your vision. It is through the support of others that you will thrive. When you build healthy relationships, you will feel more comfortable speaking up. Your opinions will be valued, your ideas challenged in a healthy way, and your confidence will soar.

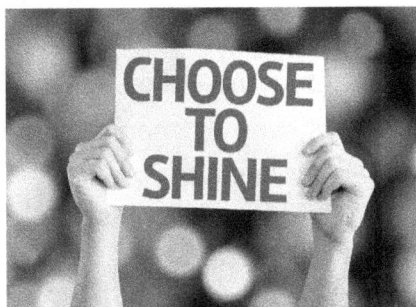

At some point along this journey, you will notice people who are where you used to be. Be kind to them, support them, and pay it forward. Lifting others as they climb is not just the right thing to do; it's an act of compassion that can make all the difference in someone's life.

Celebrate your success no matter how small! Success will help keep your Inner Critic in check.

I like to keep a small token with me for positive reinforcement. When something great happens, I reach into my pocket for my token. It can be a small stone, a lucky coin, a crystal, or a piece of cloth. I allow myself to fill with joy and a sense of accomplishment then, I take a deep breath and blow it into my token. The token becomes a powerful representation of many things that make me proud.

"The most common way people give up their power is by thinking they don't have any."

– Alice Walker

Chapter 4

Playing Small, Staying Quiet

The top 10 reasons people use for not speaking up are (including my own):

- I will upset people.
- I will get criticized.

- I don't know how to say something without being hurtful.
- Who do I think I am?
- All hell will break loose.
- There's no one to back me up.
- I'm only one person; how can I make a difference?
- Nothing will change, no point.
- It's not worth the trouble.
- No one ever listens to me/takes me seriously.

If I showed you my tongue, you'd see many pieces removed, one for every time I bit it. Those missing pieces used to have deep roots. They were attached to every moment of emotional pain I chose to bury, every wound I ignored and would not let heal.

As time passed, I got better at compartmentalizing my pain.

It was a good strategy until it wasn't. The more I ignored and swept under the carpet, the stronger the foundation of my suffering became. Only those closest to me were aware. I'd manage my emotions well for a while, then, then, out of seemingly nowhere, one of these deeply buried demons would get triggered and resurface. Sometimes, I recognized the trigger. Sometimes, I did not.

Every time you remain silent, you are granting permission to your verbal attacker to continue disrespecting you. Regardless of what you think or what you've done in the past, you are a human being who deserves to be acknowledged.

You are worthy of being heard!

Those who refuse to listen to you are afraid of what you need to say. That's why some folks want you to remain silent. As long as you continue to stay small, they triumph.

Speaking up is not about winning; it's not about who's right or who's wrong. It's about being respected enough to be heard, a painful truth to acknowledge. Being in an atmosphere where you can speak your mind and your truth means that you are in an environment where you are respected.

Please take a good look at the people in your life who listen and another look at those who don't. Are the ones who don't listen worth protecting? Keeping them comfortable is a high price to pay. You'll be paying with your sanity and dignity until you have nothing left. How long can you keep that up?

For the record, let me clarify the difference between staying silent when emotionally or verbally attacked and picking & choosing your battles. The empowerment you feel in each of these situations is the distinction.

Parents and spouses alike know what happens when you get on someone's case for *everything* instead of strategically selecting the behavior you want to influence. Remembering the mileage you get from praise and appreciation is a good thing. Giving people "positive strokes" can be a natural behavior because of upbringing when love and support surround you. If that wasn't the case for you, this is not about placing blame. You have an invitation to acknowledge the source of your nurturing instincts and make strides to modify the behavior if necessary.

When you are frustrated, hurt, or angry, it's human nature to revert to the behavior you know best. You'll need time for this transformation to occur and become a habit.

It's equally important to celebrate your successes.

Everyone is capable of reacting under pressure. When this happens, acknowledge what occurred and make amends where necessary. Eating crow is never tasty but will go a long way in relationship building.

When shifting your communication style, make a conscious effort to begin with, praise. Start slowly to ensure it's received genuinely. Practice with a lot of people.

Getting people accustomed to receiving your praise will build their trust.

Where do you start? Practice the behavior you want others to use with you. When you help others play BIG and shine for who they are, you will do the same. The more you encourage others to be authentic and speak up, the easier you will find it to speak up. Before long, the process will become natural. People talk when they feel safe.

Be the cheerleader you want to have, and over time, you will find yourself surrounded by people who support your transformation and continually encourage you to grow. As they appear, you may wonder where all these people were hiding. The truth is when you are ready, they come.

Just for fun, let your imagination run wild for a few moments and step into playing BIG. Consider how fantastic life can be with no holds barred. Dare yourself to dream outside your current comfort level and take a risk.

If you're interested, I have a great meditation to help. It will open you up to feeling empowered and supported in a way you have never felt before. If you are interested, email "Ideal Life Meditation" in the subject line to Hello@MTflower.com, and I'll send you the link to download it.

"The question isn't who is going to let me; it's who is going to stop me."

-Ayn Rand

Chapter 5

I'm Ready To Talk. Now What?

B efore you begin speaking your mind, consider how you typically communicate for a moment. If you want to be acknowledged, describing your feelings by attacking and blaming won't work. It will take courage to recognize the position you are in right now is because you allowed it to happen. I'm sorry to be so blunt, but this is critical to understand before you can gauge how well your message will be received. Please be patient with me and let me explain.

Regardless of what has happened to you, there were at least two options in front of you at the critical juncture leading down the road to your current circumstance.

It's easy to claim you had no choice, but it's not true.

There are always choices; the consequences we don't like steer us in one direction over another. Reactions become induced by anger and self-defense. Exhaustion also makes people easy targets; being depleted makes it simpler to surrender. Still, a choice was made.

The sooner you own your options, the sooner you can communicate in a way that better ensures you'll be acknowledged.

One of the most common phrases we hear in a relationship is "You made me…" Even if you have a knife to your throat, you still have the choice to fight or surrender.

Intimate relationships are most susceptible to the "You made me" argument. When you are near one another, it can be challenging not to let what your significant other has going on make an impact on you. Sometimes, you react out of empathy, or perhaps exhaustion keeps you compliant.

My husband and I are so mentally, emotionally, and energetically connected that he can "feel" me before I walk into the room. His energy will overwhelm me if I am exhausted and not paying attention. Fortunately, we have a relationship of mutual respect. Therefore we can openly speak our minds and work our misunderstandings out in record time. I invite you to take a closer look at some of your choices when you feel you have no choice.

Hindsight is a powerful teacher.

Moving back to accountability. Now that you've looked at your choices (or at least considered looking at them) and their relation to your current circumstances, perhaps you can see where things went a little crazy. A new perspective is always most useful when you are ready for it. Sometimes the wound is too fresh, even if that's the case for you, I invite you to explore this exercise:

Name An Incident or Event That Provoked You To Act With Minimal Or No Thought:

_____

_____

_____

_____

_____

How did you react?

_____

_____

_____

_____

_____

_____

Why did you react this way?

_____

_____

_____

_____

_____

_____

Do you recall the visceral reaction your body had? Where was this in your body?

_____

_____

_____

What has happened since?

_____

_____

_____

_____

_____

_____

If it happened again, what was your reaction the second time?

_____

_____

_____

_____

Have you taken any action yet toward shifting that response? If so, what?

_____

_____

_____

_____

List another alternative.

_____

_____

_____

Once armed with this information, you will better understand your feelings. When you understand your feelings, you'll better explain them without emotion. In conversation, you can acknowledge what happened without placing blame. When you take responsibility for your actions or reactions, chances are it will catch the other person off guard, especially if they are used to being blamed.

Feeling blame is half the reason people don't hear us.

Once someone feels blamed, their defenses increase, and their listening ability decreases. The other half is many people don't know how to get to the point. Many don't understand how to communicate with someone who has a style different than their own. It's almost like speaking an entirely different language. Let me further clarify communication techniques.

People are primarily visual, auditory, or kinesthetic learners.

Retaining the attention of a visual person is very different from that of an auditory or a kinesthetic person. Visual people tend to look up when contemplating an answer;

they may speak rapidly, and they usually have a lot of energy. Use visual words to help this learner *see* your message by developing pictures through your language. Use phrases like, "How does this look?" "Can you see…" or "Is this clear?" or "Can you imagine how this will …" Additionally, glancing upward will help them feel at ease.

Retaining the attention of an auditory person is very different from that of a visual or a kinesthetic person. Individuals who process by listening tend to look side to side when contemplating an answer, and their eyes tend to follow their ears. They will turn to see where the sound originates if they hear something. They also tend to speak slower than a visual person. Use auditory words and phrases like, "Does that sound good to you?" Are we in harmony on this?" "Shall I speak more directly about the facts and statistics?" or "This machine is twice as quiet as the one you now have."

Additionally, using your voice to hold the auditory learner's attention will be helpful. Change your tone, volume, pitch, and speech rate to verbally emphasize and enhance your points. They will pay as much attention, if not more, to how you speak as to what you say. Stories are powerful when communicating to an auditory person.

Retaining the attention of a kinesthetic person is very different than an auditory or a visual person. Kinesthetic people tend to look down when contemplating an answer and are very connected to their feelings. They can also be known to move around a bit as they process a question. This learning style will understand you best by *feeling* your message. Use words and phrases like, "Are you comfortable with this?" "How do you feel about that?" or "Do you need a more concrete example?" Let them know you care about their feelings; it's important they know this.

Additionally, they prefer to meet face-to-face. Kinesthetic learners crave the feeling this communication delivers. It's also helpful to match their body language; this will put them at ease.

Most people do not know what type of learning style their partner or spouse is. Here's a quick way to find out. Ask them to tell you about a childhood memory. A favorite holiday or Halloween costume will get them thinking. Pay attention to what they do with their eyes. If they look up, they are dominant visual. If they look from side to side, they are dominant auditory. If they look down and start moving their body, they are primarily kinesthetic. People are usually a combination of styles, however, knowing the dominant style will help you significantly in getting your message heard.

What happens when we cannot put our finger on how we feel?

Truth be told, there have been many times I felt something but wasn't able to explain it. I just knew I was feeling bad.

The next time you cannot describe what you're feeling, refer to these categories for assistance in understanding what's going on. Don't be surprised if a lot of words jump out at you. This process will help you break down a complicated situation into more manageable pieces.

You cannot eat an elephant all in one bite, so it's unreasonable to think you can tackle a huge amount of emotional stressors all at once.

Take one step at a time.

You may also notice the progression of feeling better as you move from one list of descriptors to the next.

Feeling Apathy or Something Similar

- Defeated
- Despair
- Discouraged
- Bored
- Failure
- Hopeless
- Indecisive
- Indifferent
- Lazy
- Lost
- Powerless
- Overwhelmed
- Spaced out
- Unfocused
- Worthless
- Listless
- Don't care
- Don't matter

Feeling Grief or Something Similar

- Anguish
- Betrayed
- Cheated
- Despair
- Helpless
- Abandoned
- Heartbroken
- Hurt
- Ignored
- Longing
- Neglected
- Mourning
- Regret
- Sadness
- Tormented
- Tortured
- Unwanted
- Unloved

Feeling Fear or Something Similar

- Cautious
- Defensive
- Apprehensive
- Embarrassed
- Horrified
- Hysterical
- Panic
- Paralyzed
- Scared
- Suspicious
- Trapped
- Irrational
- Tense
- Vulnerable
- Need to escape
- Cowardice
- Insecure
- Nervous

Feeling Lust or Something Similar

- Compulsive
- Craving
- Frenzy
- Greedy
- Horney
- Impatient
- Lascivious
- Misery
- Oblivious
- Obsessed
- Possessive
- Reckless
- Ruthless
- Voracious
- Wicked
- Must Have it
- Over indulgent

Feeling Anger or Something Similar

- Belligerent
- Caustic
- Defiant
- Explosive
- Aggressive
- Frustrated
- Jealous
- Livid
- Mean
- Resentment
- Smoldering
- Spiteful
- Stubborn
- Hatred
- Hostility
- Violent
- Willful
- Furious

Feeling Pride or Something Similar

- Clever
- Complacent
- Critical
- Disdain
- Gloating
- Isolated
- Narrow-minded
- Never wrong
- Righteous
- Selfish
- Stoic
- Uncompromising
- Unyielding
- Vain
- Judgmental
- Dogmatic
- Cool
- Aloof

There will always be a possibility you may not get to express what you want due to geography or death. When this occurs, I encourage you to refer to the previously mentioned categories and write a letter. Mail the letter if you can, burn it if you cannot. Afterward, celebrate the courage it took to get your feelings on paper.

If you can meet in person, it may be necessary to read to your listener if you are worried you'll forget certain parts. Do whatever it takes to get in front of the person you need to talk to about the issue. You have the courage. I know you do! If the other party will not listen, mail the letter and let go of the outcome.

Before you speak to the other party, **please remember this**:

You Are Not Responsible For Anyone Else's Actions Or Reactions To Your Statements.

Your listener will take what you share and do many things with it. You have **no control** over this. Most people do not speak up because they fear an unpredictable outcome. Even if you know this person intimately, you cannot predict precisely how they will react.

Chances are you will present your feelings in a way your listener is not accustomed to hearing. Please remember you are not responsible for their responses.

You have no control over anyone but yourself. Treat yourself with empathy, compassion, and care. It takes courage to be true to you. Communication will be a never-ending exploration worthy of your time and energy. The more you unveil with every exploration of this process, the stronger and more relaxed you'll become.

You *will* get better the more you practice.

Be gentle with yourself.

It takes courage to explore what you're feeling, convey your feelings, and sit patiently while the other person processes.

Consider choosing an activity before this conversation, so if you feel uneasy afterward, you have something to take your mind off things and not panic because the other person is still processing. Remove the opportunity to allow your mind to go to unhealthy places; it will be a great gift.

Say what you need to, don't overanalyze, and don't rush the response. Some people need time to process before they can give you an answer.   Everyone processes differently, which may differ from how you absorb information.

Consider how long it took you to connect with your feelings; don't forget you had tools to assist you. The categories you used to pick your emotions from are priceless. If the other person does not have these tools at their disposal, give them the benefit of the doubt and some time.   You can also consider sharing the list of emotions you experienced.

"Impart as much as you can of your spiritual being to those who are on the road with you, and accept as something precious what comes back to you from them."

- Albert Schweitzer

Chapter 6

The Vibe

There is one more important factor to consider before having your first conversation: the "vibe" you'll be putting out when you're talking. Your vibe is a combination of your words, body language, and the signal you emit as a result of your feelings.

The vibration we emit is the one thing most people don't pay attention to when communicating, whether it's one-to-one or from a stage. What you feel and think and how you carry your body will send a stronger message than your words.

For example, consider someone minding their business when a hostile person enters the room. Without hearing a word, you can pick up on someone's vibe by their facial expression and how they move their body. You can feel their presence well before they speak.

To counter the point, let's look at a dynamic, energetic, and uplifting person. Imagine you're at a networking event and see someone walk into the room with a big smile. This person moves confidently, speaks graciously, and is welcomed warmly. Most of us want to meet this kind of person because we are intrigued.

Someone who can carry him or her in such a manner unconsciously helps us feel better by making a positive impact at a distance. We can feel the positive vibe they are giving off and want more.

Your vibe will speak volumes!

It's important to understand because when faced with having an awkward conversation, it's essential to prepare yourself mentally, emotionally, and physically to keep your energy in check. Writing out what you want to say covers the mental preparation.

There is no shame in reading from a piece of paper. You don't want to feel bad afterward because you left something out. If you read from the paper, try to look up frequently to understand the other person's reactions. Take your time and remember to breathe. If you notice the other person crossing their arms over their body, they have probably gone into defense mode. Take a moment and ask them what they are thinking, hearing, or feeling. Remind them your intent is not to make them feel bad but to convey your feelings. It's so important to take responsibility for what you are feeling and not place blame.

Prepare emotionally by reviewing the feelings you were having up to this point and remembering you cannot control the other person. If you go into fear mode, think back to when you were empowered and go into another room, place your hands on your hips, or stretch your arms out to the side. Making your personal space as large as possible will help you feel larger than life. Another body position to play with is clasping your hands behind your head and pulling your elbows back as comfortably as possible. Another version is sitting in a chair and putting your feet up on the desk or table.

Be mindful of your shoulders; they will try to curl in if you're not paying attention. If you have to exaggerate sticking your chest out to train your shoulders, have fun with that until you find the right balance.

The goal is to believe you are capable, worthy and deserve to be acknowledged. If time permits, set yourself up to have a series of small successes in the days preceding the conversation. Build the muscle.

Practicing all of these techniques regularly will strengthen the positive vibe you give when communicating.   Additionally, consider keeping your heart open and feel compassion for the other person. Chances are they are hurting too.

*"Life is 10 percent what happens to me
and 90 percent of how I react to it."*

– Charles Swindoll

Chapter 7

Learning To Let Go

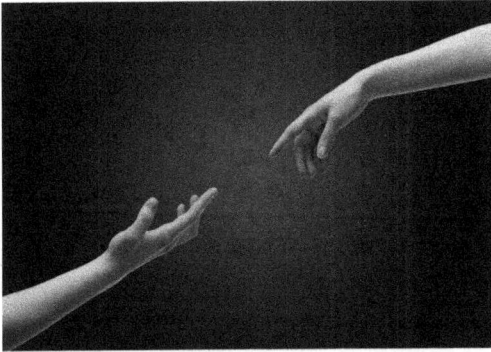

Now that you are better prepared to express yourself, it's time to practice non-attachment to outcome. Non-attachment is a life-long practice. With time, you will master this and endure much less stress. "Let go and let God" is an expression you may have heard before. Whether you are religious or not, the concept is a good one. Letting go of what we have no control of is just about the healthiest thing you can do for yourself.

Every situation has a variety of potential outcomes, each dictated by things in and out of your control. All you can do is focus on what is in your control. Things such as:

- How you show up.
- How you let things roll off your back.
- How things get under your skin.
- How you perform.
- How you ask for help.
- How you receive help.
- How you treat people.
- How you express gratitude.
- How you convey appreciation.
- How you show respect.
- How you show compassion.
- How you express your opinions.

I invite you to take a look at each of these statements and consider your answers. You may not have paid much attention in the past to how you behave or react to each of these; you probably had no reason to.

For those of you feeling brave, consider asking a couple of people close to you how they see you approach each topic. It can be a fantastic learning experience when you receive feedback from a place of appreciation and non-judgment. What a beautiful practice!

If the person you're asking this of feels safe, they will answer you openly and honestly. Consider in advance how you will reward them for their sincerity. Keep it as a surprise. This simple action will make them feel valued as a person and friend.

Before we get too far into letting go, we must examine why we resist. The thing about holding on we never pay much attention to is the power of ownership.

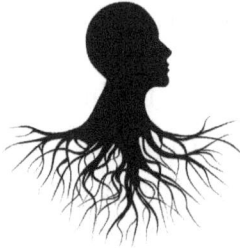

People have been taking things from you all your life. Siblings were grabbing your toys, parents who took freedom, lovers who broke your heart and took your innocence, employers who took your joy, the government taking your money and responsibilities taking your time. The one thing that can never be taken from you is your reaction/response to a situation. No one can take your anger or your resentment from you unless you surrender it. Unhealthy as these things are, you own them and don't easily let them go without provocation.

It's the attachment to our stories that keeps us believing we can or cannot do something. As Henry Ford said,

"If you believe you can or you cannot, you are right."

The problem with unhealthy stories is the "runaway train factor." Once we get going, it can be challenging to stop them. We can get addicted to sympathy. Additionally, if someone hears the story more than once, they may remind us later, making it a challenge for us to move on.

I've set a 3 "tell" limit for myself. After that, it's time to move on - especially if it's unpleasant. I give myself three times to get it out of my system. If I still feel like the situation needs work by that time, I'll focus on the problem and work it out. Only then can I start placing my energy in more productive places.

There are a lot of times this requires taking a cold, hard look at why I'm behaving a certain way and why I'm not letting go. The discomfort of moving through this is worth the effort, even though it's uncomfortable. I often have a series of things connected, it's like going down a rabbit hole.

Have you ever watched a film and cried so intensely it caught you off guard? It's as though the movie triggered every other time in your life you needed to cry and suppress it. The film can be a key to unlocking what you need to release.

If you're with someone who doesn't like to see you cry, give him or her a heads-up when you feel the tears coming. It's better to let the emotion flow while you have the chance.

I've had people attempt to make me laugh when I needed to cry. I didn't tell them I needed to cry, so they proceeded to cheer me up. All I wanted was to go through a box of tissues. Clarifying what you need is a healthy practice to adopt.

Let's talk about the release.

Letting go happens at three different times and in three different ways.

I use being in a relationship as an example. You've been dating someone for some time now, and things aren't going as well as you'd like. You feel you're being taken advantage of or disrespected, and you've finally had enough. You decide to end it. The emotion kicks in once you make a rational decision and your heart aches.

It's easy to go back to the good qualities this person had and how they stood above the rest (best lover, gracious, generous gifts, etc.) You may question if you were too hard on them. You may feel kicked in the gut or want to curl up in a ball and cry; you may feel betrayed or like your heart has been ripped out. The release ends here for many.

The most unrecognized and perhaps the most important place you need to let go is, in your gut.

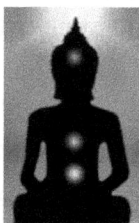

The solar plexus is where your energetic connection to the person resides. Failure to cut this tie may result in a repeat performance, either with the same person or a similar person down the road. As unhealthy or uncomfortable as this type of person is, the energy is familiar, and you can, with some certainty, predict what will happen in some situations. If they do this, then this will happen. If they do that, then this will happen. There's comfort in predictability.

I remained in an unhealthy marriage to an alcoholic for 18 years for this reason. The unknown of being on my own with a young child was more frightening than the stress I'd become accustomed to balancing.

I've conducted hundreds of sessions with people who never let go energetically in their gut. Watching the shift in someone who has been through the trenches and come out the other side is one of the most beautiful things I've had the privilege to see.

It's taken me a long time to master the art of this release. I'm fond of writing things down and burning them. I've released the same thing "to the fire" over and over again because I hadn't realized the solar plexus was a component of the release. I was often so consumed by the emotion of the situation that I wasn't ready to let go entirely. Now, I practice checking in on all three levels when it's time to move beyond something.

I suggest doing this release under the supervision of someone who can hold space for you in a sacred setting and offer you very specific guidance. Setting a clear intent is paramount.

Interested in more information on a group gathering to foster some release work? For yourself or hosting an event for friends or family who are ready to step into more fulfilling relationships, we can help with new levels of growth. Our release ceremonies are gentle and loving. For more information on our services or how to foster healthier relationships, check out the blog section on the website, www.MTflower.com

"Control your own destiny or someone else will."

- Jack Welch

Chapter 8

Calling All People Pleaser's

The key takeaway here is: You're not responsible for another person's actions or reactions! You cannot make someone do or feel anything. You can intimidate, but you have no direct control over another person. Think of it as trying to keep puppies in a box or a toddler who just learned how to walk still. It's not happening.

Whether you are a people pleaser or a recovering one, this topic will strike a chord. Please proceed with compassion.

Think of the top instances you didn't speak up due to concern over how someone else would react.

1. _____

2. _____

3. _____

Although you believed you knew how a person would react, how accurate was that assumption? Knowing people well and projecting how they'll perceive us is based on historical data, not necessarily fact. The reality is that regardless of how well you know someone, you never know how someone feels. Using historical data to make assumptions is dangerous; if you continue to determine how someone will act or react in advance, you'll be keeping a lot of information to yourself because you won't take action.

Somewhere along the line, you may begin to believe you were responsible for another person's actions or reactions. Has this belief created new drama, more enabling, and stress? If you answer truthfully, is it time to stop assuming that responsibility?

Our mothers often told us, "If you don't have anything nice to say, don't say anything," and it stuck. It's a complicated script to rewrite. I'm not advocating harsh words. I'm advocating personal expression to reduce stress.

I have often sacrificed my piece of mind to protect another person's feelings. Why did I care more about their suffering than my own? I didn't know any better.

Sometimes, I wasn't familiar with feeling powerful yet; other times, I didn't feel like enduring confrontation. I'm also a Libra;

this sign represents a peacekeeping role. Sometimes, I simply don't want to hurt another person's feelings. I used to treat others how I liked to be treated; eventually, I realized why that didn't always work.

Here's a challenge to the "do unto others" rule. Imagine if you are outgoing and love attention, and you show praise to an "introvert" the way you like to be appreciated. How do you think they'd react? An "introvert" will not enjoy being the center of attention. The same applies in the opposite direction.

If you're more comfortable pleasing others than speaking up, I challenge you: please come to terms with knowing you are worthy of being heard and respected. It's your right to be heard; no one can take it away.

Transforming surrender into confidence is possible.

Find other people who have mastered the

skill and create a strategy to step gradually into it. If that's not your style, diving right in will not produce the lasting results you want. Building on a series of small successes is your best bet.

Setting the bar too high without preparing yourself for small successes along the way will drain your enthusiasm. Feeling like you've accomplished a task, small or large, as you work toward the larger goal is essential. Understanding the human psyche and the need to feel good sheds light on why hitting a small attainable goal inspires you. Setting lofty goals is admirable; however, you have a recipe for stress without the proper strategy.

We are a society of people with active inner critics; we find more reasons to criticize than to praise ourselves. The "all or nothing" model puts up unforeseen roadblocks. When you don't recognize your progress, you get frustrated. You may be the type who rarely celebrates success and immediately moves on to the next task.

Going through such an important process as recognizing why you'd rather please other people instead of honoring your needs requires thought and coming up for air. How often do you come up for air in general? Are you exhausted?

If you feel that you never got the recognition you've always hungered for growing up and nothing you do is good enough, you're not alone.

Are you pushing yourself well beyond the point of exhaustion because you've always had to work harder?

Is your body so used to the challenges of being driven, that you thrive under such pressure? Exhaustion will take the edge off the emotional pain, but it's only a short-term fix. This pace cannot be maintained in the long run, and the time required to repair the damage will take longer than you'd like. Did I mention this will happen at the most inconvenient time?

There's never a wrong time to start taking better care of yourself despite what anyone tells you.

I've helped many people come to terms with this behavior in a loving and gentle way. You can shift out of this by taking a stand for yourself. Life is too short to live in the shadow of something you are not. I believe in you and your ability to shine. Who wants to start shining brighter?

"Too many of us are not living our dreams because we are living our fears."

-Les Brown

Chapter 9

I Don't Want To!

How many times have you done something regardless of whether or not you wanted to? Were you afraid of what would happen if you spoke up and refused to perform?

For example, hosting a holiday gathering takes a lot of time, a lot of money, and a lot of energy. Have you ever had a guest who doesn't fully appreciate it?

As women, we often take on the responsibility of keeping the peace and the family together. We don't want to be responsible for breaking tradition. We don't want that kind of guilt.

If you sit down and think about how much you do that you have no desire to do, you may be surprised at what comes up.

What are the top 3 things you do out of obligation that no longer bring you joy?

1. _____
2. _____
3. _____

I'm not suggesting you take immediate action on this list. Instead, I'm inviting you to recognize what's been happening. It's up to you where you take it from there. The simple act of bringing awareness to this will help you realize how draining these actions have been.

When you are ready to take action and endure a slight resistance to achieve your peace of mind, you will feel so liberated. You'll wonder what took you so long.

It's easy to feel trapped in a routine because we're too exhausted to consider how the other side of the fence looks. Plenty of times, I had no bandwidth for a simple conversation because it involved me thinking about something outside the realms of where I was stuck.

I know it sounds crazy, you have an invitation to get off the hamster wheel, but you can't imagine what you'll do once you get off! When you're so busy you operate on autopilot, there's an odd comfort in that because minimal thought is involved. The problem is you are draining yourself beyond your reserves.

Emotional exhaustion is always more challenging than physical exhaustion.

When you are exhausted from a long day of physical work, you can drop on the couch, sink in, watch a movie, or stare into space perfectly content. When you are emotionally exhausted, a script is running in the background. You cannot easily escape the drama and often have trouble sleeping or relaxing. I'd take physical exhaustion over mental ANY DAY!

It's important to consider why we keep doing things we don't want to do. Sometimes, the consequence seems more challenging than the act itself. Other times, we simply don't have the bandwidth to shake things up.

If you are already busy, making a little time for such an endeavor can be a challenge. There have been plenty of occasions when I couldn't listen to something that suggested action, even if it were years later. At such moments, I was under so much stress; it's incredible I didn't completely break down. There simply wasn't room in my life for anything to go wrong, much less change.

As simple as the following exercise sounds, I'll be the first to tell you it won't be easy if you're already overwhelmed. If you're in overdrive mode, you may find that any shift in behavior (aka slowing down) can produce guilt. As crazy as this seems, it's true. Start small and be gentle with yourself.

It is possible to begin setting aside small chunks of time to remain committed to fulfilling. These little windows of time may look like taking 3 minutes in the car before you get out to go into the office or walk in the house at night. It may look like taking a few extra minutes in the bathroom. You may be laughing at the bathroom suggestion, but I've heard plenty of women say that's the only moment they have peace.

When overwhelmed, it's important to take the time wherever you can get it and not be sorry about it. If you are so accustomed to constantly giving to everyone else while keeping yourself last on the list, there will be a little retraining required to get everyone else up to speed on your plan. Or you can go on strike.

It's important to share where you are and what you are feeling with those closest to you. An unexplained shift in your behavior will raise questions and cause false assumptions. You will only create more stress. When you tell your family, friends, etc., what's going on, be mindful of stating facts and not placing blame. You can also ask if others in the family feel the same. It's possible that you are not alone. If this is the case, you can develop a plan as a family.

If you suspect you'll face resistance, consider the potential reactions you'll receive and your responses. So many times, people are too exhausted to think things through, and then they get into trouble. Half the challenge is to be ready for a variety of potential scenarios. When you prepare for various outcomes, you'll be less intimidated and ready for almost anything because you've thought things through.

Sincerely asking for help will get people's attention.

Once upon a time, asking for help to me meant showing a sign of weakness. I lost a job once because I was too proud to ask for help. In the long run, I was better off; however, it still took me years to improve the skill of asking. Practice makes progress; perfection isn't a realistic expectation.

Women get caught in the mindset of exerting twice the effort for a fraction of the recognition. When others count on you, asking for help is difficult. Some of you have learned to stand your ground in the face of business adversity, but when it comes to your personal life, that's another story.

Asking for help can be tricky business. First, you must admit you need something; be prepared for someone else to perform the task similarly, but not exactly how you would. Lastly, you must be ready for people who are not available.

It is difficult to say which circumstances carry the most significant risk; it's entirely subjective, based on the task. Risk at some level is not foreign to you, but it's different when it's personal. When you need help the most, it can be devastating not to receive it. The last thing you want is to become discouraged by a legitimate refusal and eventually stop asking for help altogether.

New skills take some time to develop.

Remember to cut yourself some slack. The intent is to set you up for success, not mediocrity or failure. Begin with something trivial to build your confidence in asking. Eventually, you'll be comfortable, and a pleasant byproduct is that you'll get better at receiving in the process.

Often, your resistance to asking for help can run so deeply that you'd rather suffer in emotional or physical turmoil than admit you could use a hand. With women's success in many arenas, there is still a lot of room for improvement in the "get help" department. What if we looked at asking for help as delegating? There is no shame in telling your family you need them to help pick up the slack.

You may think, "Ok, I'll ask for help at home, but I know how that will go!" Here's something to consider when you want someone to do something for you.

Motivation Is An External Force

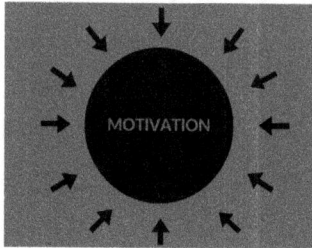

Inspiration Moves People From Within

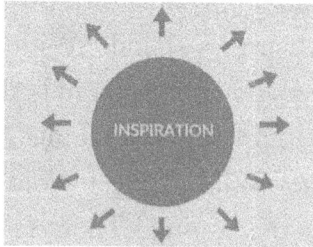

Being inspired produces a visceral reaction within you. It makes a spark and draws you to something or someone you want to emulate.

When you are inspired, you experience a shift in your consciousness, awareness, or physical body and feel the need to act strongly.

The key to inspiring another person is sincerity.

People are terrific at picking up a vibe from someone genuine versus someone who is looking out for him or herself. Work on creative ways to inspire others to help you instead of motivating them. The impact will last much longer. People will take notice.

Imagine becoming so successful at inspiring others that what you need from people eventually becomes effortless. It's about leadership, not about ego. You are setting an example; it's about successful communication, and ultimately, it's about personal leadership. This behavior will cross over into every realm of your life and produce fantastic results and, ultimately, less stress.

"Where you stand, depends on where you sit".

-Nelson Mandela

Chapter 10

Children Are Meant To Be Seen
And Not Heard

H ere's a classic. If so many adults clearly can recall being told as children that they are "meant to be seen, not heard," I must ask, at what point do individuals become adults who can speak up? What if it never happens?

I took a long time to learn the value of picking and choosing battles. I never felt I had good examples to follow. In my 20s and 30s, many of my battles felt like a loss before they ever began, so I kept quiet.

Some people remain silent because they are choosing their battles wisely. Others like me were in a constant pattern of defeat when we were younger.

Just because you've settled for something in the past does not mean you must continue to.

I cannot stress enough the importance of speaking up before a situation gets beyond a manageable level.

If you're accustomed to keeping quiet, you may get worked up in the heat of the moment and then calm down later. Things blow over. When things return to the status quo, you may put the situation behind you, hoping it won't happen again. Then you forget until the next time.

When "next time" comes, every emotion you felt initially returns again. The only problem is that not only are you feeling the emotions of the past, but you are beating yourself up for letting this happen again. For such a dangerous compounding effect, it's, unfortunately, a very familiar pattern.

It's much easier to sweep something under the carpet than address and attempt to fix it. I swept so much under the rug that I had speed bumps and tripped.

How we deal with things is developed early on, usually before age 10. The people we spend time with further reinforce these patterns. It's very common for people to go from one controlling situation to another. Being controlled is familiar. Imagine it as an invisible magnet. You cannot see the force, but you feel it and step into situations that "feel" familiar. It's unconscious. If someone points it out to you, you'll deny it. However, you'll wonder how you missed it once you see it.

Adults do not consciously reflect on their childhood as the catalyst for poor skills and misunderstood behavior; however, a script runs in the background.

We have a lot of scripts running in the background; everyone does. These are the filters in which we see the world. There are far too many filters and scripts to discuss here, but it's essential to know how these stories shape how we show up in life. I'm still working on plenty of my own; there's always another layer.

Here's a quick example: let's say you were brought up in a household where money wasn't a topic of discussion; chances are you will be secretive about your finances.

If conversation was encouraged at the dinner table as a youth, then you probably encourage your children to do the same.

The dinner table is a great "safe zone" to get things out if agreed upon in advance. You're doing well when you can express yourself over a meal and keep eating!

If silence was a pattern in your childhood, you might find comfort in silence now because it's all you know. No judgment, merely data on behaviors become a habit.

As children, we automatically find safety in structure and permission. Although children may resist or even resent the direction, it's reassuring that someone cares about you and your welfare.

There are always cases of rebellion where a child refuses to conform and exhibits the opposite behavior a parent desires. Some kids become successful in business and life because they won't settle for being told they cannot do something. Regretfully, that has always been one of my biggest motivators.

I've changed careers to prove a point when someone told me I couldn't do something. Not one of my brightest hours; truthfully, it was some of the most painful 13 months of my employment history. However, I learned a lot in the process and am grateful to recognize the pattern.

The rambling story is one of my unhealthy communication traits that can be carried over from childhood. I'm much better now, but GEEZ, it was terrible!

Some people need "warming up to" before getting into the meat of the conversation. Others want you to get right to the point.

If you need to tell a long story before getting to the point and are communicating with people who aren't that style, therein lies the problem. You may get cut off, calls aren't returned promptly, or people will always be too busy to talk.

Chapter 5, "I'm Ready To Talk. Now What?" refers to the various communication styles to get a clearer sense of the style of the person you communicate with most frequently. Shifting your style slightly to match theirs will significantly impact your effectiveness.

The most effective communicators have the ability to "tune in" to their audience, whether it's one person or a thousand people.

This skill takes practice; don't give up after a couple of attempts. It took decades for you (and me) to become proficient in your familiar communication style; you cannot expect to change overnight. Keep with it and you'll notice improvement!

*"I am not a product of my circumstances.
I am a product of my decisions."*

-Stephen Covey

Chapter 11

Who Do You Think You Are?

How many times have you heard the question, "Who do you think you are?" Could you answer it?

Congratulations if you did. How often have you found yourself unable to respond to the question of who you think you are? For me, it was many times. I heard this "question" frequently during my first marriage. Truthfully, looking back, I realize I may have asked this question of others a lot in my younger years.

For some people, this can be another great motivator. This can be one of the most significant deterrents to confidence for others.

When someone has a delicate sense of self, a harsh word can easily undermine their confidence. Words can impact people; however, the vibe people convey while communicating is more powerful.

The energy behind your words carries a powerful force you cannot see.

Your energy reflects how you feel at the moment and about the person you're talking to. Your energy may even reflect an unconscious judgment. Beware of the hidden combination of your "vibe" and a few harsh words. You can create an unintentional cascade of negativity on your unsuspecting recipient.

When timid people hear the question, "Who do you think you are?" they can be easily thrown off their game. They can be distracted, disillusioned, or worse, they can be devastated. It's bad enough when we question ourselves. When someone else challenges us, it can become humiliating.

With practice, you can courageously answer this question. If you haven't asked yourself this question in a while, or ever, for that matter – maybe now is a good time.

Here's a little challenge for you:

What are 3 things that make you unique?

1. _____
2. _____
3. _____

Now ask 3 people what they know is unique about you.

1. _____
2. _____
3. _____

Everyone needs a little soul food. If you cannot make the time to appreciate these fine qualities in yourself, how do you expect others to?

Be clear on the difference between feeling good and feeding the ego.

Don't be afraid to acknowledge your value!

Acknowledgment is not egotistical. It's an exercise in feeling good and building your confidence. When ego steps in front of being heart-centered, that's when problems can arise. This practice is intended to raise your level of appreciation and empowerment to serve others by recognizing your strengths.

Please don't confuse confidence with arrogance.

Imagine confidence as coming from a heart-centered place of service; it's not ego-based.

Confident people can be very humble and give when they intend to serve. Arrogance is confidence running a rye and manifesting as ego. It's also a reflection of pain.

Usually, an arrogant person is very insecure and uses this behavior as a protection mechanism. When someone keeps people intimidated or in fear, there's less chance anyone will get close enough to see what's happening. It's a proven fact that many relationships fail because one person doesn't feel comfortable exhibiting who they are.

It took me a while to understand that aggressive, malicious people are in pain. We put up walls to keep people out and feel safe.

Self-defense takes on many forms; from silence to shutting people out; my defense was the wall I built around me. The tool that brought my wall down was love.

When I married the second time, I had deep wounds and trust issues. Add to that the fact that I married my husband within six months of meeting him (too long a story to tell here). If you asked me who I thought I was then, I'd have told you I was independent, strong, and determined. These strengths quickly became faults in a relationship. I got what I wanted, yet I didn't know how to handle it. Although I was and am to this day a very spiritual person, that doesn't mean I am indifferent to my demons.

Fortunately, my husband was patient and loved me completely. He could see my pain and held space for me to grow. He helped me see things as they were in a non-emotional way, which helped me on many levels. Mark still helps me acknowledge my progress when I forget how far I've come.

Clearing my past has been paramount in helping me work with others.

Every client teaches me more about the human condition and how we hold on to pain. I committed long ago to help people heal so they can connect to their gifts. Finding your voice and sharing your story has never been more critical than it is right now.

I challenge you to answer truthfully the question, "Who do you think you are?" Once you come to terms with that, the next step is to take this "knowing" to another level and start "feeling" who you are. When you transform from a thinking being to a feeling being, your habits and behaviors source from a deeper place. People will feel this shift. They may not be able to pinpoint what has changed, but they will sense it.

Think of this as a fun, fact-finding mission. Once you come up with a series of answers, look at each answer and consider why this makes you who you are. You will gain an in-depth perspective of how far you've come and may see some patterns you want to change. We are not talking about an exercise in judgment but an objective look at who you are and how you got where you are. Imagine this as a springboard to the next level of your personal development. You'll be fully prepared to answer the next time someone asks you that question.

"What we achieve inwardly will change outer reality."

–Plutarch

Chapter 12

Graciously Receiving

Graciously receiving can be one of the most challenging things we work on throughout our adult lives. For those who are nurturers and selfless, receiving may be a foreign concept. Mastering the art of graciously

receiving is easier than you think.   It
requires two simple words.

Thank you.

As tempting as it may be to explain away a
compliment or undermine one, all you need
to master the art of graciously receiving is
to say "Thank you" and **BE QUIET**! Let
me warn you: this is easier said than done.

I've heard countless speakers get off the
stage and refute compliments or make
derogatory   remarks   about   their
performance before anyone can say
something positive. When this happens, it
can be an unconscious intimidation
behavior to provoke praise. It can also be
the Inner Critic working overtime.

When we feel bad, people often give us
empty compliments to help us feel better,
regardless of how truthful the statement is.

You can probably imagine a time or two
when this has happened; perhaps a bad

hairstyle, a wardrobe malfunction, or something stuck in your teeth. It's not until the event is over that we discover the disturbing truth of what people saw. When you can laugh at your faux pas, cheers to you! If you're not there yet, may I suggest you work on that – you'll be a lot less stressed.

When you watch how people receive praise, you can see how well they accept or avoid the compliment. I've explained away more compliments than I care to admit to, from someone liking my clothing to honoring courageous action.

I used to degrade wardrobe compliments with the admission of consignment store purchases. I made the jacket or skirt unworthy of praise because of where I bought it, which now seems ridiculous. I'm getting better at receiving praise from others; it's an ongoing process.

If praise is a foreign concept to you, consider giving it. The act of giving praise will not only help another person, but it will also help you feel good in the process.

You can also practice smiling. It takes fewer muscles to smile than it does to frown. When you begin smiling more easily, imagine radiating a peaceful vibe to everyone around you. When I feel terrific, I envision my energy radiating from my entire body, helping people feel good.

You can also practice absorbing the vibe from something you appreciate, like a beautiful flower or a sunset. The key word here is absorbing. It's important to note this because when you are in the presence of a person you appreciate, you'll want to absorb their energy instead of taking it. Think of it as receiving.

Almost everyone has experienced being in the presence of someone who drains your energy. Someone negative or needy is probably unaware of the energetic impact made on other people. Most people who drain your energy don't realize they are doing it. It's been a pattern to get what they need, to be fed, or to get attention. You cannot pull yourself away from these people during a conversation.

Feeling compassion for these individuals is important because they are in pain. Offer them a compliment and dismiss yourself gracefully from the conversation.

Graciously receiving is a muscle you build over time. Once you begin using it, a new world will open up. You'll notice how many people appreciate you and acknowledge you, and, in time, you will embrace your skills in a whole new light. You'll also see your powerful impact on others with a few simple words.

"Nothing is impossible, the word itself says 'I'm possible"!

-Audrey Hepburn

Chapter 13

Breaking The Cycle

Speaking up is a matter of dignity. It's about honoring your feelings, respecting yourself, and believing you have every right to feel like you do. If you don't honor yourself by speaking up, you cannot expect anyone else to acknowledge you.

Everyone goes through challenges and questions their worthiness. During low self-esteem, examining your thoughts and actions is easy. Even the most confident people question themselves. You aren't alone.

When you know someone is going through a tough time and overreacts to a situation, they are in a lot of pain and keeping it to themselves. The person may not possess the communication tools or have the experience to get the results they want by any other means. They only know how to achieve an outcome by being louder, dominating, or creating fear. Their default reaction is the sum of their experience; it may be the only way they know.

Moving out of reactive behavior is easy to describe but complicated to initiate. Proactively shifting a habit takes dedication and perseverance. It's a matter of learning new coping and communicating mechanisms and then having the courage to apply them consistently. It's also getting the people around you used to your new behavior.

One of the reasons you may be "stuck" in an unhealthy pattern is that those around you have become accustomed to who you are. For you to change requires them to change. Not always an easy sell. Not to mention, many people lack the courage or the desire to make these changes. They cannot see what's in it for them.

The inspiration drawing you to consider making a change begins deep within you. Often, a chord is struck you cannot explain; you only know something has happened and are no longer comfortable where you are.

The internal shift is the difference between motivation and inspiration. Inspiration comes from a flame within you; it makes you want to take action and continue taking action regardless of the consequences. You believe so intensely, and what you're doing, you cannot be stopped.

Truth be told, breaking the cycle of silence takes tenacity and determination. The temptation to resort back to familiar patterns will be there. The people who have become accustomed to your communication style can predict, to some extent, how you will act or react to certain situations. Changing the game will require them to get accustomed to a new you. They may not like it and question your motives. Be honest and sincere.

The first cycle you will be breaking is your own. You are breaking patterns of action and reaction, acceptance and denial. Be patient; the journey will be well worth it.

You'll have to ask yourself how committed you are to this process and how patient you are willing to be with your progress. This type of transformation has no specific timeline. There will be spontaneous moments and challenging times. I can say one thing for sure: the experience of developing self-respect by speaking up is never a bad thing. I believe you are worthy.

Evaluating your motives in advance will help strategize your response to unsupportive feedback. Clarifying why you are speaking up will be the foundation upon which everything moves forward.

On the next page, you'll find some thought-provoking questions to help you gain clarity on why finding your voice is important and what your intent is when you find your voice. Since there are a lot of questions, don't attempt to answer them all. You can close your eyes, place your finger on the page, and see where it lands.

When you are ready to explore these questions, give yourself a time limit. At the end of your session, acknowledge yourself for making the time and reward yourself. I'm sure you'll want to return to the list repeatedly. You'll come from a slightly different perspective whenever you explore these questions.

Personal Fulfillment

- What will it take for you to feel complete?
- What's the first action you must take to bring you one step closer to feeling whole?
- When are you willing to take this action?
- How can you reward yourself by taking this action?
- What will it take for you to feel worthy of being heard?
- Do you need help with this?
- Who can support you in this process?

The Power of Your Beliefs

- What will it take for you to know I believe in you?
- What will it take for you to feel like your story matters?
- What needs to happen for you to believe in yourself as I believe in you?
- What do you need to stay inspired?
- Can you keep a phrase or a photo of this in your wallet, your car or put one on the bathroom mirror?
- What do you need to feel like you are fully living your life?
- How attainable is this?
- What must you do to begin the process?
- Can you commit to a tiny daily action to bring yourself closer to fully living your life?
- What is the one positive thing you believe about yourself?
- How long have you known this?
- If you stopped thinking this at one time in your life, what caused that?

<u>True Happiness</u>

- When is the last time you felt truly happy?
- What do you need to be happy again?
- What's getting in the way of that?
- How will life be different when you feel truly happy?
- Can you accept that you are worthy of happiness?
- Can you make a list of the top 5 or 10 moments in your life when you were happiest?
- What has changed since you were happy then?
- What small action can you take every day to bring yourself joy today?

<u>The Power of Friendship & Compassion</u>

- What does your best friend tell you when they want to cheer you up?
- Why does this work so well?
- What do you tell your best friend when you want to cheer them up?
- Why does this work so well?
- What's the most important thing you learned from your best friend?
- Who do you feel the most compassion for and why?

Life Lessons

- What's the most important thing you learned in your 20s?
- What was your happiest moment in your 20's?
- What's the most important thing you learned in your 30s?
- What was your happiest moment in your 30's?
- It is the most important thing you learned in your 40s?
- What was your happiest moment in your 40's?
- What's the most important thing you learned in your 50s?
- What was your happiest moment in your 50's?
- What's the most important thing you learned in your 60s?
- What was your happiest moment in your 60's?

Immediate Family

- What's the most important thing you want your child to learn from you?
- What's the one thing you believe your child has learned from you?
- What's the most important thing you've learned from your kids?
- What's the most important thing you learned from your spouse?
- What's the most important thing you want your husband or wife to know?
- How often do you tell them this?
- What's the most important thing you learned from your pet?

<u>Moving Through Pain</u>

- What's the most important thing you can learn from being alone?
- Who is the person that hurt you the most?
- Do they know they hurt you?
- If they don't know, can you tell them?
- Can you imagine a sense of relief from getting that weight off your shoulders?
- What have you learned from this person?
- Can you find in your heart to thank them for the lesson even if they've hurt you?
- What is your deepest emotional scar?
- Can you forgive the person you believe caused this pain?
- Do you still feel resentment toward this person?
- How long have you felt resentful?
- If you were no longer resentful, where would you be focusing your energy?
- How has pain been your teacher?
- Who do you most want to have a conversation with that has passed?
- What would you say to them?

- Can you write to them?
- Can you believe reading your letter allowed well be heard by them?
- Who's the person you least want to have a talk with?
- Why?
- How much better would you feel if you said what you felt regardless of their reaction?
- What needs to happen for you to have this conversation?

Whatever has come up in the process of reviewing and answering these questions, please realize these reactions are coming from a place of fear.

Fear comes from uncertainty. Many of these topics are left untouched because it's been easier to ignore the pain than understand it and work through it to be free.

If you've been in pain for a long time, I get it's familiar, and joy may be entirely foreign. Most things can be worked out when discussed from a place of compassion and trust. Remember the

importance   of   not   blaming;   taking
responsibility for what you feel is important.

When you shift how you communicate, people
will take notice. Reinforcing the good in others
will go a long way.

**Telling someone how much you appreciate
them will produce powerful
results over time.**

You will inspire others to do things for you
simply by regularly expressing gratitude and
appreciation.

When you make praise a habit, you'll quickly
notice the difference between people offering
you genuine accolades and those with a hidden
agenda. You will also notice this when
observing other people offering praise.

It's akin to getting a new red car. Now you
notice how many red cars are on the road before
you are oblivious.

Friends, associates, and family members who
are not around you will always ask what you've
been up to because you look better, appear
happier, and are more confident.

The world will see you differently because you see the world differently.

"Believe you can and you're halfway there."

-Theodore Roosevelt

Chapter 14

Public Speaking

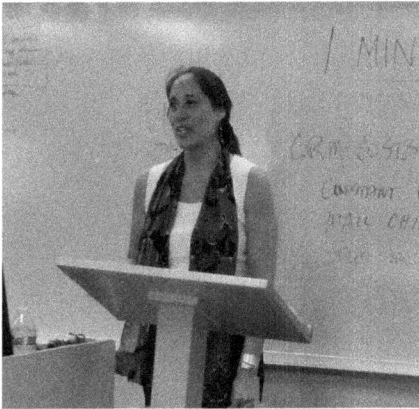

My goal throughout this book was to help you see the value of speaking up throughout every aspect of your life. When you are more comfortable speaking up in familial situations and declaring with confidence what you feel and why, speaking in all other areas of your life will fall into place.

If you are already comfortable speaking in public, my goal is for you to be more confident in your personal life.

Most people who speak professionally go into one of three categories. Either they tolerate it, love it, or HATE it. Those who hate it don't see the need to learn the skill, much less master it. These folks will find every excuse to avoid doing presentations at work, in their civic group, or in business organizations.

Those who love it make it look easy and will jump on almost any opportunity to share a story or teach.

Those who tolerate it will perform when necessary but don't pretend they enjoy it.

If you are required to speak as part of your profession, yet you are intimidated when speaking in front of supervisors, please consider your unique contribution.

Regardless of your seniority, you bring unique skills to your position. You have a unique perspective on problem-solving. This makes you an expert, even in the presence of senior-level management. Hold your own by being authentic and believing in your skills. Practice the power poses to make yourself larger than life. Envision the accolades you'll receive afterward. Another trick I like to use is visualizing three different outcomes.

The first result is, "It'd be great if this happened..." The second outcome is "it'd be even better if this happened!" the third result is my out-of-the-ballpark vision or "you can't make this up..."

Regardless of what happens, I always feel I did my best and will learn something valuable to apply to my next talk.

If you film your talks, here's a great tip: I like to review them three times. First, I listen (usually on the way home), then I look at the video with sound. Lastly, I watch the video without sound. Each viewing provides a unique perspective.

Although I've frequently been outspoken, I didn't always love being on the stage. Years ago, I tolerated speaking.

My earliest professional speaking recollection was an introduction I volunteered to do at a networking event in my early 20s. I was nervous. Making small talk with the attendees was a useless exercise in feeling better. Perhaps if I didn't openly declare my nervousness and proclaim I'd forget my lines, I may have remembered my lines. Everyone who heard me attempted to reassure me I'd be okay. The only problem was I wasn't convinced. I forgot my lines. My earliest lesson was seeing how powerful my thoughts and words were, and it was memorable.

Prophecy and visualization are tools for success and tools for failure. Only you can choose how you want to use them.

Visualizing the reactions of an audience is a practice adopted long ago. I also imagine giving my all, shining my brightest, and saying what I need to say when it needs to be said.

When I realized the time I had invested in writing talks was nothing more than an exercise in creative writing, I stopped spending so much time writing talks. Realizing I'd never deliver them the same way I wrote them was such a relief. Now, I do an outline and trust that I will provide what the audience needs.

I love chatting with attendees before my talk, and I incorporate those conversations into the talk. Additionally, I feel more animated and connected to the audience because there's no stress over a script. It's pretty liberating. PowerPoint is also a tool for staying on track. I use images like flashcards; a memory is evoked, and a story is told to reinforce a point. The visual people in the audience are happy, so it's a win/win situation.

For the record, PowerPoint took a little practice. I'd practice the setup in advance, using a projector and a slide clicker, running the presentation on the computer, and using a recording device. Doing a trial run to ensure everything worked correctly was a huge stress relief. I'd also timed my setup to know how much time I needed to allow at the venue. Ensure you have extra batteries, extension cords, power strips, etc. This alone will help you focus on the people attending. You will be fully present, knowing you've handled all the small details in advance.

Everyone has the potential to be a terrific speaker. If you look at people who hate speaking, it begs the question of how confident they are. Speaking opens you up and taps into every fear you've ever had about being "good enough." Speaking for the shyest is the ultimate exercise in overcoming vulnerability that can produce the best rewards.

I've always believed public speaking can be a spiritual experience.

Praise is usually in order, considering what many people must overcome to get out there, stand on a stage, and feel confident. That takes immense courage, which requires self-exploration and personal growth. It also involves accepting one's worthiness. I don't know what it is if that's not the equivalent of a spiritual experience!

Here's to your exploration of keeping it real by finding your truth and speaking it. I know you have it in you. I know you are worthy of being heard.

Every week, I have a few openings to mentor people like you to find the courage to begin the journey. During our 60-minute conversation, I'll help you see the power in your story and why it needs to be told. We will discuss an action plan to get you started so you can begin feeling worthy of indeed being heard. I'll help you see the possibility of standing tall before anyone and feeling powerful as you speak up. Email me at Hello@MTflower.com, and I'll send you the details.

Many Blessings,

Mountain Flower

"Keep away from people who try to belittle your ambitions. Small people always do that, but the really great ones make you feel that you, too, can be great."

-    *Mark Twain*

About The Author

Mountain Flower has been in private practice, helping people appreciate their life journey while transforming self-doubt into confidence since 1999. Her mission is to heal all sense of disconnection so people can live in alignment with their body, spirit, Earth Mother, and the Divine. When people remember they have support, it becomes easier for them to speak their truth and tell their story. From the ceremonies she facilitates to her mentoring clients and connection programs and her inspirational book publishing program, "Tell Your Story," Mountain Flower helps people thrive and be happier than ever.

As a Native American Medicine Woman, she has an extensive understanding of the human condition's pain and has helped thousands. She has been called a grounded, powerful presence and an inspirational leader.

Mountain Flower is an unconventional thinker and courageous implementer. In the early 2000s, the Connecticut LT Governor recognized her as a Woman of Fire.

She has presented for The United Way, The University of New Mexico Anderson Graduate School of Management, The Society for Information Management, the Southern New England Chapter of Project Management Institute, Girl Scouts of CT, and many women's and business organizations. Inquiries for inspirational book publishing are welcome at Hello@MTflower.com, or you may call her directly at 860-303-8772.

A passionate advocate for women and girls globally. She once served as a director on the board for Girl Scouts of CT and as their Board Development Chair. She has also served as the President of the Southeastern CT Women's

Network and as an Area Governor for Toastmasters International.

Mountain Flower lives in Connecticut with her husband, Wasaka, and her son. On the East Coast, she enjoys organic gardening, cooking, writing, walking her dog, and being in the company of strong women. She is also an avid hiker and horseback rider in the mountains of the Southwest.

For more information on working with Moutain Flower or bringing her in for a group event, see the event page of her website, www.MTflower.com.

Healing Through Your Story

Healing Through Your Story

medicinewoman_mountainflower

Leslie Mountain Flower Hammond